PICTOGRAMS

Graphing Pictures for a
Reusable Classroom Grid

Laura Duncan Choate

JoAnn King Okey

DALE SEYMOUR PUBLICATIONS

Cover designer: Rachel Gage
Editor: Frances Christie
Illustrator: Elizabeth Marston

Order number DS01905
ISBN 0-86651-487-2

DALE
SEYMOUR
PUBLICATIONS
P.O. BOX 10888
PALO ALTO, CA 94303

6 7 8 9 10 11 12-MA-95

Introduction

Pictograms: Graphing Pictures for a Reusable Classroom Grid is part of a series of materials from Dale Seymour Publications that is designed to help you bring graphing into your primary classroom. This volume provides nearly 400 pictures—or *pictograms*—that you can use to create a wide variety of readable and appealing graphs.

The pictograms are designed especially for use with *Graphing Grids,* a set of four large blank-grid posters that can be adapted for making wall, floor, or tabletop graphs. The correlated teacher's resource book *Graphing Primer* offers an extensive introduction to graphing techniques, reproducible pages to help students analyze and understand what they've graphed, and ideas for many enjoyable group and individual graphing experiences. Although the series is suggested for use with kindergarten through second grade students, preschoolers and older students alike can also benefit from graphing experiences using these materials.

WHY GRAPH?

Graphing is an ideal math activity at the primary level. It allows young students to relate to numbers both tactilely and visually. The reading of words is reduced to a minimum. As a way of gathering and looking at real-world data, graphing helps students relate math to their personal experiences.

Graphs provide a structure for organizing and simplifying collections of figures. This is likely your students' first experience with statistics. As they gather and graph information in the classroom and make comparisons of the data, students discover that statistics are an integral part of daily life, and that such statistics can help them draw mathematical conclusions about the world around them.

WHAT SKILLS DOES GRAPHING INVOLVE?

Graphing everyday data develops a number of different skills. At the most elementary level, students learn to identify similarities and differences. Gradually they become more sophisticated in defining the attributes of different objects. Graphing develops the ability to sort, to classify, and to place objects in one-to-one correspondence on the graph.

Making the graph itself is only the first step. Students also develop skills in interpreting graphs. They must be able to count the amounts in each category and do simple visual comparisons. Addition and subtraction skills are used as students begin to do exact comparisons. Problem-solving skills are called into play as students try to determine why certain results were obtained, whether or not those results could be generalized to a broader situation, and if the results might be used to predict future situations.

THE THREE STAGES OF GRAPHING

Students are more likely to understand graphing if we present it in three developmental stages, progressing from the concrete to the abstract.

Real graphs. At the first stage, students make *real* or *object* graphs, comparing actual objects that they place in the squares of a blank grid laying flat on a table or floor. This concrete stage lays the foundation for understanding more abstract graphs.

Picture graphs. At this intermediate stage, students graph with pictures—graphic symbols of something real—rather than with real objects. This stage forms an important bridge between real and abstract graphs.

Abstract graphs. In this third stage, students use symbols—such as X's, circles, or squares—to represent real things. This is the most abstract level since, to find meaning, students must relate each symbol back to the real object it stands for.

Beginning graphers should have the chance to graph the same set of data sequentially through all three stages of graphing. Repeated exposure to the same data in different forms will enhance their understanding of the relationship between real (concrete) and abstract (symbolic) graphs.

USING PICTOGRAMS

Pictograms are useful at all three stages of graphing. To make a real graph, you might use pictograms to label the categories, mounting each pictogram on a 3-by-5-inch card that is folded in half to stand up like a tent. For example, the pictograms for orange, grapes, tomato, cranberries, and apple (pages 25–26) could be used for labels on a real graph of "Favorite Juice," while students would indicate their responses with real paper cups.

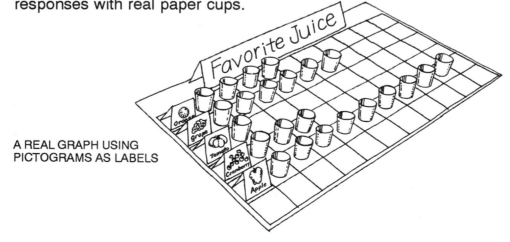

A REAL GRAPH USING
PICTOGRAMS AS LABELS

A picture graph can be created entirely with pictograms and graphing grids displayed on the wall. For example, consider how you could graph the topic "How We Get to School." You might label the categories with pictograms of a car, a bike, a bus, and a person walking (page 16), duplicated on colored paper to distinguish them as labels. Students could then mark their responses with identical pictograms that you have duplicated from this book and that they have colored, or with face pictograms (page 8) that they have colored to represent themselves.

How We Get To School

A PICTURE GRAPH USING IDENTICAL
PICTOGRAMS FOR STUDENT RESPONSES

How We Get To School

A PICTURE GRAPH USING PICTOGRAM FACES
FOR STUDENT RESPONSES

For an abstract graph, you would use pictograms only to label the categories, while students record their responses symbolically—maybe with X's or with simple gummed circles.

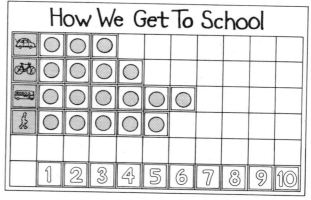

How We Get To School

AN ABSTRACT GRAPH USING
PICTOGRAMS AS LABELS

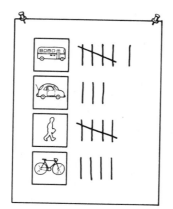

A TALLY GRAPH
USING PICTOGRAMS

The pictograms can also be used to make a tally graph. Mount them on a large blank sheet of paper for display on a bulletin board or easel, and let students use crayons, markers, or a grease pencil to make a tally mark for each response.

When you are using pictograms with the blank graphing grids displayed on the wall, attach them in one of the following ways to ensure that your blank grids can be used again and again:

Paper clip mounts. Use a single-sided razor blade or similar sharp instrument to cut along the 1/2-inch slit at the top of each grid square. Slide the tip of a plain paper clip through the slit and push down until the larger side of the clip is behind the grid and the shorter loop is visible from the front.

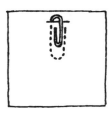

Always keep a paper clip mounted in each square. Labels and pictograms can then be easily mounted on the grid by slipping them under the clips.

Paper fastener hooks. Cut the slit at the top of each square as described above. From the back of the grid, slip a 1-inch paper fastener through each slit. Fold the longer section of the fastener flat against the surface of the grid and bend the second section into a hook shape.

To make a graph using this mechanism, simply punch a hole in the top of each label or pictogram and hang it from a paper fastener hook.

Magnet mounts. Tape the grid to a magnetic chalkboard. Use magnets or magnetic tape to mount your labels and pictograms.

Velcro mounts. Secure a small strip of Velcro to the top of each square on the grid and attach a corresponding piece to the back of each label and pictogram.

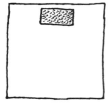

As labels for categories, pictograms are usually placed in the column of squares farthest to the left or in rows across the bottom or top of the grid. Placing the labels at the right edge (for graphing from right to left) is not recommended at the primary level, since students are still learning the left-to-right reading sequence.

ALWAYS BE READY TO GRAPH

Opportunities for graphing occur daily in the classroom, yet we often let them slip by, thinking that we simply don't have time to prepare everything needed to make a graph. That's where this series of materials can help out. With a set of reusable graphing grids and a collection of pictograms—duplicated, cut apart, colored, and stored in envelopes by subject—you can be prepared to take advantage of any graphing opportunity that comes along. The more frequently you do graphing in the classroom, the more adept your students will become at interpreting graphs and developing their critical thinking skills.

Some teachers like to create a permanent display or "graphing center" in their classrooms. This is easily done by mounting a reusable wall grid on a bulletin board under a general title such as "Read Our Graphs" or "We're Speaking Graphically!" Be sure to leave space on the grid for a specific title, written on a sentence strip, for each new graph you make. Mount the pictogram numerals across the bottom of the grid for making numerical comparisons, and use prepared or student-made pictograms for graphing responses. When you are finished with the graph, simply remove all the pictograms and sentence strip title and your blank grid is ready to use again. Store the pictograms with the sentence-strip title in a labeled envelope or file folder for use at another time.

GRAPH DONE IN A PERMANENT DISPLAY

TALKING ABOUT YOUR GRAPHS

Students should be encouraged to discuss and interpret every graph they make. Ask specific questions that require them to react to the graphed data. For example, in a discussion of the "Favorite Pet" graph you might ask:

Which row has the most? the fewest? Are any rows the same? Are there more dogs or cats? Are there more fish or birds? Are there fewer cats or birds? How many dogs are there? How many fish? How many *more* dogs are there than cats? How many *fewer* birds are there than dogs? How many pets are there altogether? Which is the most popular pet? If another class made a graph to answer the same question, would the graph be the same?

After such a discussion, you might leave each new graph on display for several days, allowing students to make additional discoveries on their own. As students become more comfortable with the concept, you will find them asking questions and discussing the graphs together during free time, even without your direction.

ABOUT THIS BOOK

The pictograms in this book are organized into three broad categories: Getting Acquainted, Favorites, and Science. Within each category, the pictograms are clustered by theme.

You'll find nine pictograms per page, each identified by a simple word or phrase, with a number of questions at the top that suggest a variety of topics students might graph. An index at the back of the book lists individual pictograms, as well as general categories, to help you locate what you need for any particular graph.

You can duplicate these pictograms as many times as needed for use with your own students. They are designed to be colored. Occasionally, unlabeled pictures are provided for making your own custom pictograms—as for eye color (page 9), time of day (page 11), and ice-cream flavors (page 31).

The three categories offer a wealth of topics for classroom graphing experiences, as suggested below.

Getting acquainted. Each year teachers and students undergo a period of becoming acquainted with one another. This period is also one of learning to recognize and respect similarities and differences within the group. Graphing activities are a perfect way to explore the unique characteristics of each individual and foster a sense of self-worth while also building a sense of belonging through shared common experiences.

"GETTING ACQUAINTED" GRAPHS

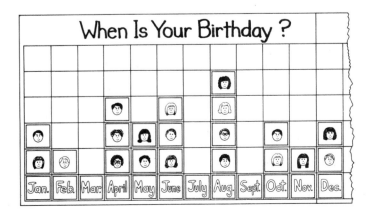

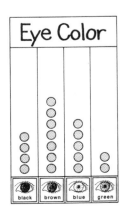

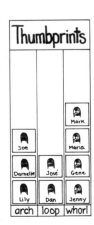

Favorites. Graphing individual preferences—such as favorite color, favorite snack, favorite pet, favorite sport, favorite vegetable, favorite dinosaur—encourages students to express their own opinions as well as to be aware of and respect the opinions of others. These graphs can also be used to make group decisions such as "What game should we play at recess?" or "Which song shall we sing today?"

"FAVORITES" GRAPHS

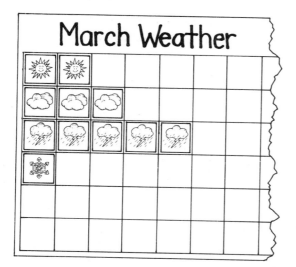

Science. Many science topics lend themselves especially well to graphing. Among the possibilities are recording weather types; classifying by such categories as animal groupings, leaf shapes, and cloud types; and testing objects for buoyancy and for magnetism. Graphing helps students organize information in a way that naturally leads them to draw conclusions and form theories about the results of their experiments or observations.

"SCIENCE" GRAPHS

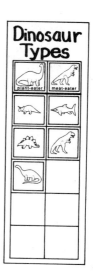

Since it is practical to graph information about all curricular areas, graphing experiences can be integrated throughout the entire school day. Some graphing activities can be ongoing cumulative projects—recording, for example, number of teeth lost each month, birthdays, and daily weather. Graphs can also be used to chart certain aspects of your daily routine, such as attendance, lunch or milk orders, transportation to and from school, and time spent at different activities.

Although the nearly 400 pictograms in this book cover a wide variety of topics, there could easily be hundreds more. You and your students can make your own pictograms to fit any topic by using photographs, magazine cut-outs, stickers, old workbook or coloring-book cut-outs, or your own drawings.

YES • NO • MAYBE • NUMERALS

Are you buying hot lunch today?

Will you share today in show-and-tell?

Are you going out of town for the holiday weekend?

TEACHING TIP: Use numerals to number the columns across the bottom of a graphing grid.

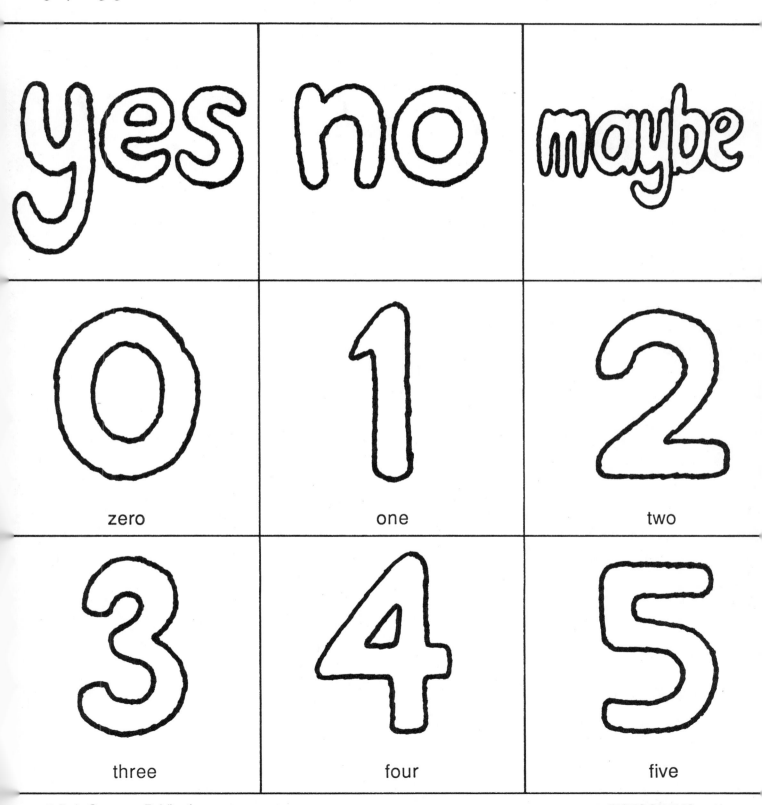

yes	no	maybe
0	1	2
zero	one	two
3	4	5
three	four	five

NUMERALS

What is your favorite number?
How old are you?
Which are the odd numbers?
Which are the even numbers?

6	7	8
six	seven	eight
9	10	11
nine	ten	eleven
12	13	14
twelve	thirteen	fourteen

NUMERALS • BOY • GIRL

What numbers are in your home address?

Are you a boy or a girl?

Do you have a brother or a sister?

TEACHING TIP: Have students add hair to turn the smiling face into a self-portrait for responding on Getting Acquainted graphs.

fifteen

sixteen

seventeen

eighteen

nineteen

twenty

boy

girl

DAYS OF THE WEEK • DAY • NIGHT

On what day were you born?
On what day is your birthday this year?
What is your favorite day of the week?
Which do you prefer, day or night?
When do you go to bed? When do you get up?

Sun.	Mon.	Tues.
Wed.	Thurs.	Fri.
Sat.	day	night

MONTHS

In what month were you born?
What is your favorite month?
What is your least favorite month?

Jan.	Feb.	Mar.
April	May	June
July	Aug.	Sept.

MONTHS

How many school days are in each month?
How many days does it rain each month?
In what month is your favorite holiday?

January

February

March

April

May

June

MONTHS • LUNCHES

What type of lunch do you like best?
What type of lunch are you eating today?
What type of lunch do you eat most often?

		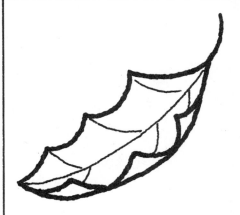
July	August	September

October	November	December

hot lunch	lunch box	brown bag

HAIR COLOR • HAIR STYLE

What color is your hair?
What is your favorite hair color?
Guess which hair color is most common in our school.
Do you have long hair or short hair?
Is your hair curly or straight?

blond	brown	black

red	gray	long hair

short hair	curly hair	straight hair

EYE COLOR

What color are your eyes?

What is your favorite eye color?

What color are your best friend's eyes?

What color are your father's/mother's eyes?

TEACHING TIP: Use the extra eyes for other colors—such as yellow (a cat's eyes).

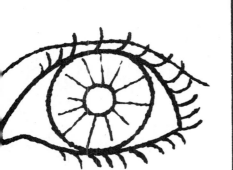

blue

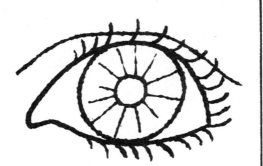

brown

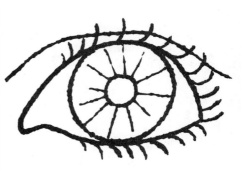

green

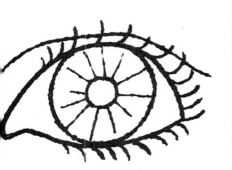

black

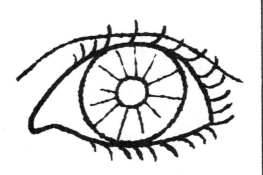

gray

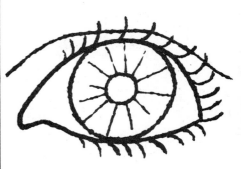

hazel

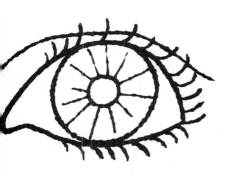

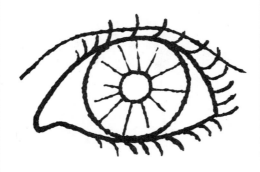

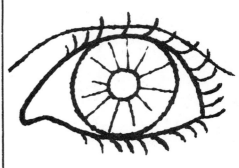

TEETH

Have you lost a tooth?

How many teeth do you have?

What color is your toothbrush? What color is the toothpaste you use?

Do you use toothpaste from a tube or a pump?

What is the name of toothpaste you use?

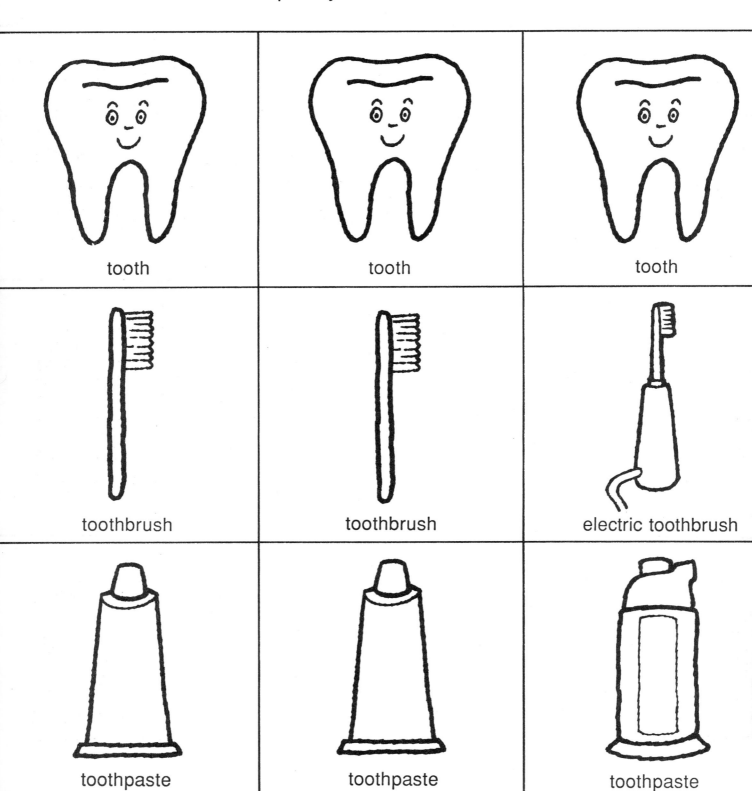

tooth	tooth	tooth
toothbrush	toothbrush	electric toothbrush
toothpaste	toothpaste	toothpaste

CLOCKS

When is your bedtime?

What is your favorite time of day?

At what time do you wake up? eat breakfast? eat dinner?

TEACHING TIP: Duplicate the clocks and fill in different times, both standard and digital.

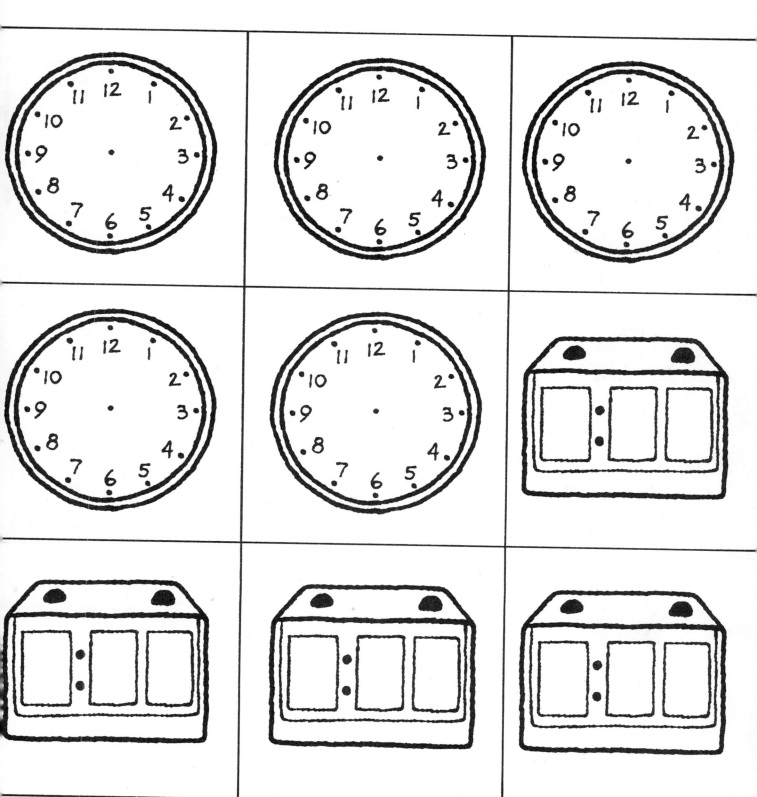

DWELLINGS • FINGERPRINTS

Where do you live?

TEACHING TIP: Have students draw pictograms for any home-type not included.

What kind of thumbprint do you have?
How many of your fingers have loops?

TEACHING TIP: Have students wet their fingertips to see the prints better, or use a stamp pad to make their fingerprints on paper.

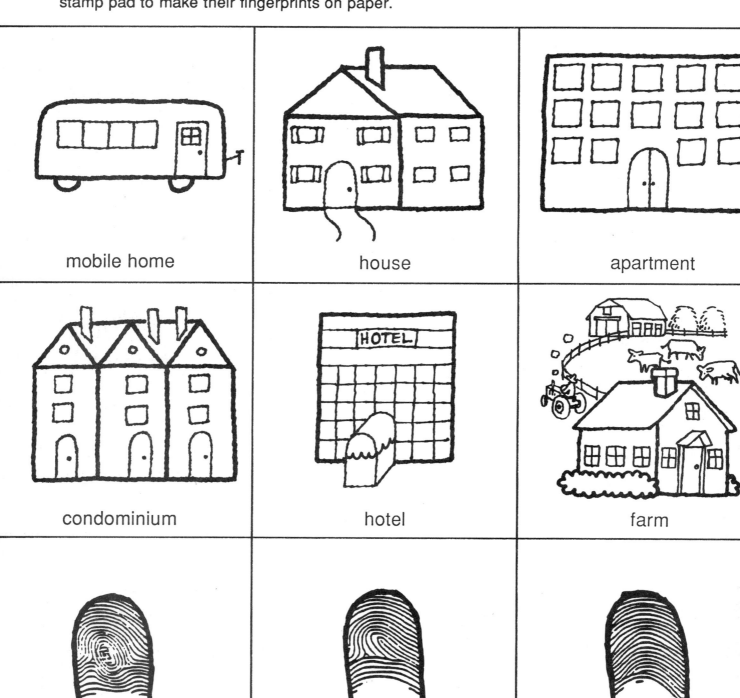

mobile home	house	apartment
condominium	hotel	farm
whorl	loop	arch

EARS • TONGUES • HANDS • THUMBS

Do you have hanging or attached earlobes?
Can you curl your tongue?
Are you left-handed, right-handed, or ambidextrous?
When you clasp your hands together, is your right or left thumb on top?

hanging earlobe

attached earlobe

curled tongue

flat tongue

left-handed

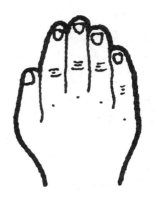

right-handed

ambidextrous

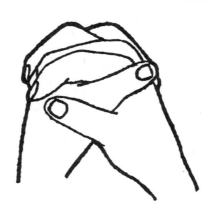

right-thumbed

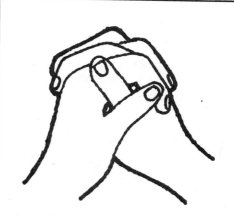

left-thumbed

PETS

What pet do you have?

What is your favorite pet?

What pet would you like to have?

What pet would you **not** like to have?

fish

cat

dog

hamster

bird

rabbit

rat

turtle

guinea pig

PETS

Which pets could live with you?
Which pet is the cuddliest?
Which pet is the most unusual?

| snake | horse | lizard |

| ants | parakeet | goose |

| hermit crab | tarantula | snail |

TRANSPORTATION

How did you get to school today?
How do you usually come to school?
What is your favorite way to come to school?

walk

bike

car

skateboard

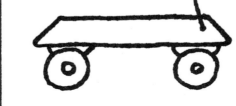

scooter

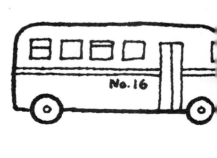

bus

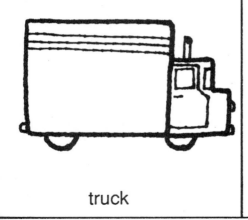

truck

motorcycle

taxi cab

TRANSPORTATION

How did you travel on your last vacation?
If you were going to see your grandparents, how would you get there?
What is your favorite way to travel?
What way of traveling would you most like to try?
What way of traveling would you **not** like to try?

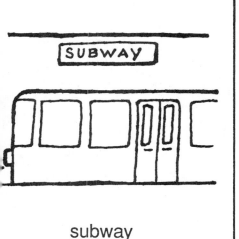

subway

train

airplane

hang glider

parachute

hot-air balloon

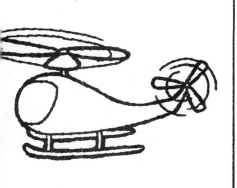

helicopter

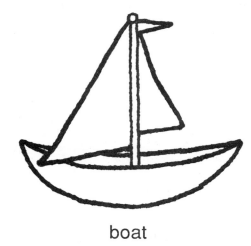

boat

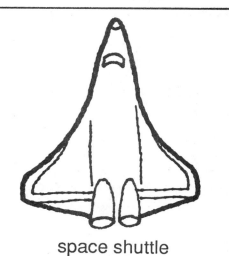

space shuttle

FEELINGS

How did the story make you feel?

How do you feel about school? How do you feel about recess?

When someone won't share with you, how do you feel?

How does your birthday make you feel?

TEACHING TIP: Use the blank faces to depict other types of feelings.

happy

sad

angry

excited

scared

indifferent

sleepy

GLASSES • SHOES

Do you wear glasses?

How many people in your family wear glasses?

What kind of shoe are you wearing?

What is your favorite kind of shoe?

What kind of shoe is most comfortable?

 glasses	 no glasses	 boots
 sandals	 sneakers	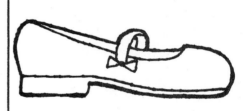 dress shoes
 thongs	 slippers	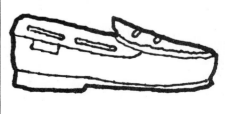 slip-ons

SHOES • CLOTHING

Do your shoes tie, buckle, have Velcro, or just slip on?
Are you wearing short sleeves, long sleeves, or no sleeves?
Are you wearing anything with stripes?
Are you wearing something with a zipper?

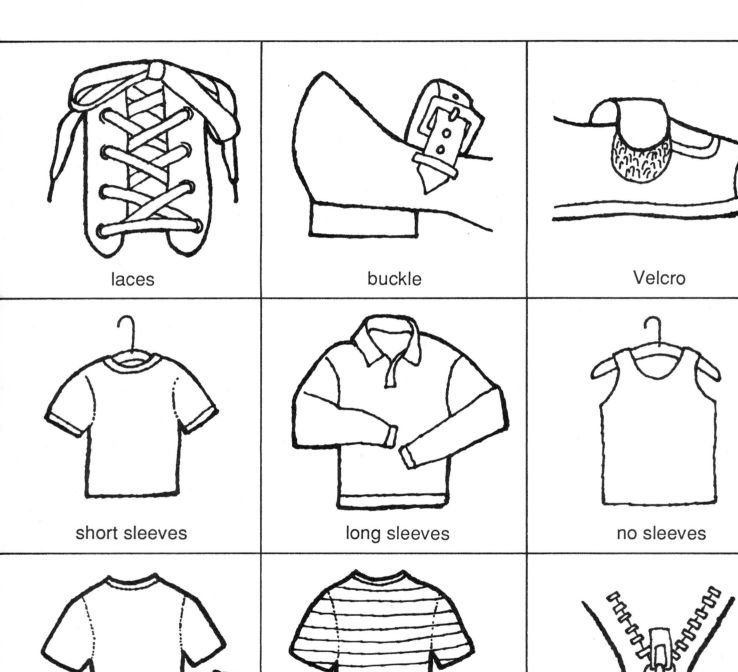

laces	buckle	Velcro
short sleeves	long sleeves	no sleeves
no stripes	stripes	zipper

CLOTHING

Are you wearing something with buttons?
Are you wearing a belt?
Are you wearing anything with pockets?
How many pockets do you have today?
What do you like to wear best?

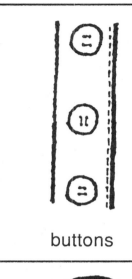

buttons

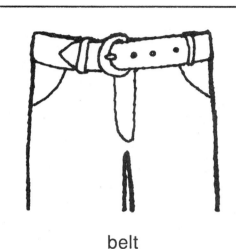

belt

elastic

pockets

no pockets

pants

shorts

skirt

dress

CLOTHING

Are you wearing short socks? knee socks? tights?
Did you bring a coat to school today? a jacket? a sweater?
How many of you are wearing jeans?
Coming to school, did you wear gloves? mittens? neither?

jeans

coat

sweater

short socks

knee socks

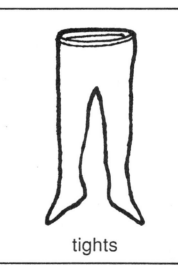

tights

bare feet

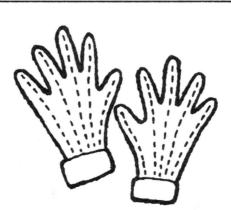

gloves

bare hands

CLOTHING • HATS

Are you wearing a ring?
Dld you wear a hat to school today? If so, what kind?
Which hats do you have in your family?
What kind of hat do you like best?

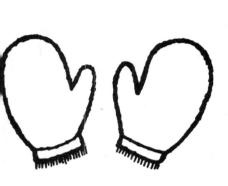

mittens

ring

ski mask

hard hat

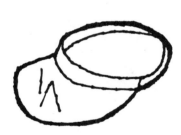

sun visor

stocking hat

straw hat

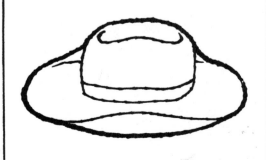

Western hat

baseball cap

COLORS

What is your favorite color?

What color is your favorite t-shirt? favorite shoes?

What color is your favorite fruit? favorite vegetable?

　　　　favorite ice cream? favorite juice drink?

red

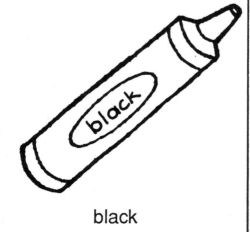

yellow

green

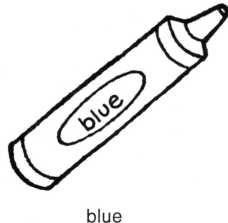

blue

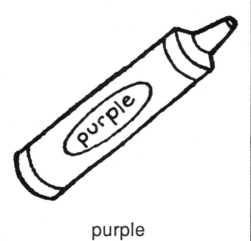

purple

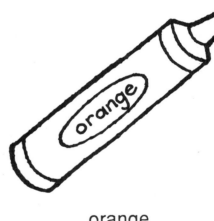

orange

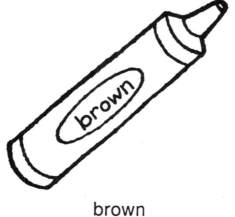

black

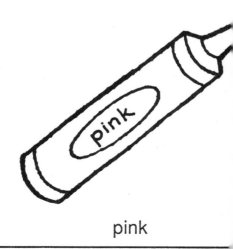

brown

pink

COLORS • FRUITS

TEACHING TIP: Duplicate the blank crayon for any colors not included on page 24.

What is your favorite fruit?
What kind of fruit juice do you like best?
What kind of fruit do you eat most often?

grapes

orange

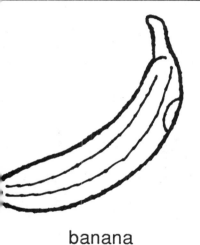

banana

apple

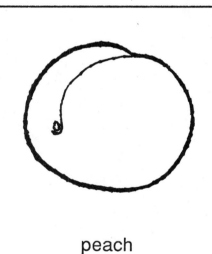

peach

pear

cherry

strawberry

FRUITS • VEGETABLES
What fruits would be good in fruit salad?
What fruits are good in a pie? in yogurt?
What fruits have you tasted? never tasted?
How can we sort these fruits? (color, size, season)

pineapple

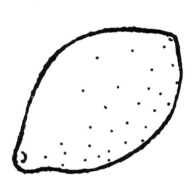

lemon

plum

cranberries

blueberries

blackberries

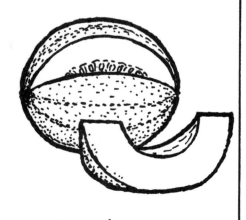

melon

tomato

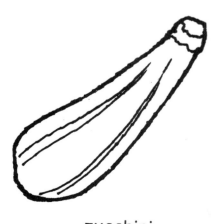

zucchini

VEGETABLES

What is your favorite vegetable? least favorite vegetable?
What vegetable do you eat most often?
What vegetables do you eat raw?
What vegetables do you eat cooked?

lettuce

cauliflower

pumpkin

spinach

broccoli

cabbage

peas

green beans

potato

© Dale Seymour Publications

VEGETABLES

What vegetables are good in salad?

Which vegetables have you tasted? never tasted?

Which vegetables grow above ground? below ground?

Let's sort the vegetables by color.

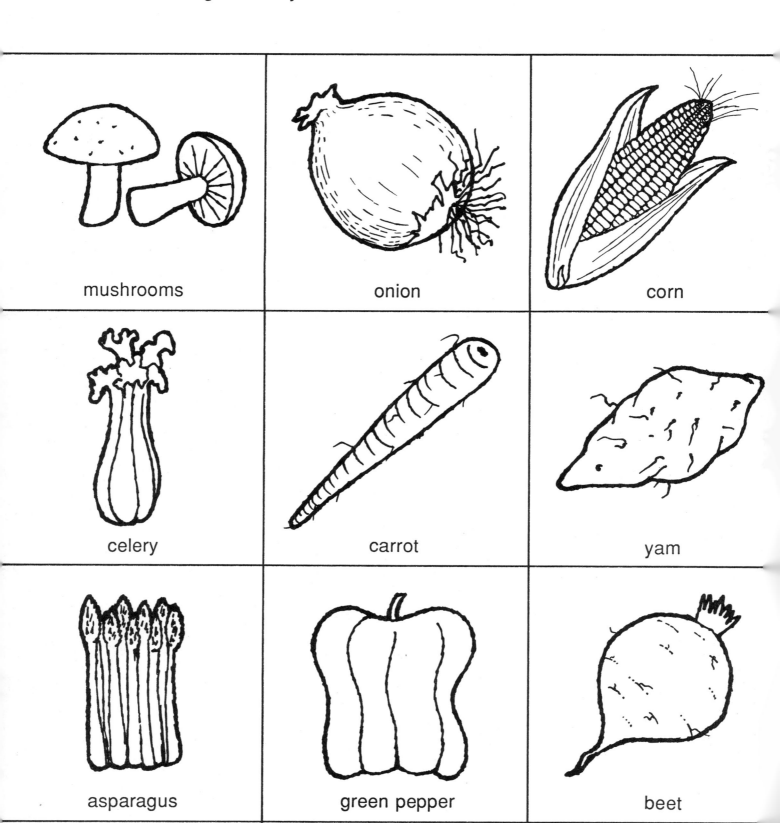

mushrooms

onion

corn

celery

carrot

yam

asparagus

green pepper

beet

SNACKS

What is your favorite snack? your second favorite?
Which snack do you eat most often?
Which snack is most nutritious?
Which snack did you bring today?

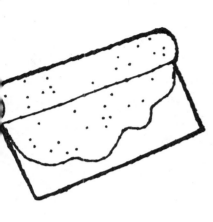

fruit roll

popcorn

raisins

granola bar

cheese and crackers

yogurt

nuts

sunflower seeds

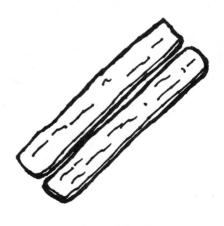

beef jerky

DESSERTS
What is your favorite dessert?
What is the most special dessert?
Which desserts have you helped make?
Which dessert do you have most often?

cake

pie

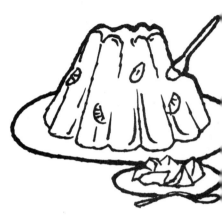

Jell-O

donut

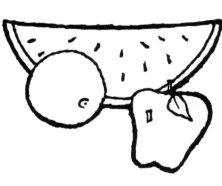

fruit

candy

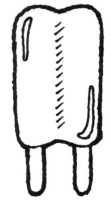

Popsicle

pudding

cookies

ICE CREAM

What is your favorite flavor?

Which flavor do you like best in a shake? in an ice-cream soda?

Which flavor do you like with birthday cake?

Let's sort the flavors by color.

TEACHING TIP: Use the blank cones to name and color other popular flavors.

chocolate

vanilla

strawberry

BEVERAGES

What is your favorite thing to drink?
What beverage would you like for a class party?
What do you drink with your meals?
What will you drink with lunch today?

TEACHING TIP: Use the empty glasses to name and color other beverages.

milk

chocolate milk

water

soda pop

lemonade

juice

cocoa

PASTA • CRACKERS

What type of pasta do you like best?
What types of pasta have you eaten?
What shape of cracker do you like best? What flavor?
Which crackers do you eat most of?

pasta wheels

elbow macaroni

macaroni

pasta shells

pasta spirals

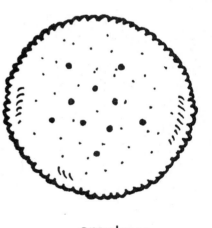

crackers

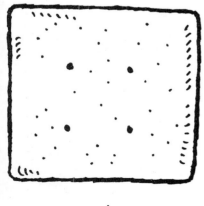

crackers

crackers

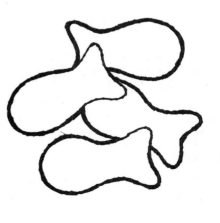

crackers

NURSERY RHYMES

What is your favorite nursery rhyme? your second favorite?
Which nursery rhymes can you say?
Which nursery rhyme would you like to act out?

 Hickory Dickory Dock	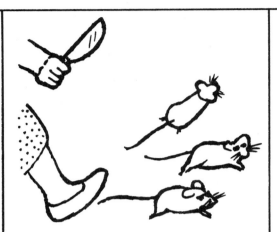 Three Blind Mice	 Baa Baa Black Sheep
 Old Mother Hubbard	 Jack Be Nimble	 Little Miss Muffet
 Jack and Jill	 Little Boy Blue	 Mary Had a Little Lamb

FAIRY TALES • BOOKS

What is your favorite fairy tale?

What is your favorite book?

What fairy tale would you like to perform as a play?

TEACHING TIP: Duplicate the blank books to name other student favorites and stories you are reading in class.

Cinderella

Hansel and Gretel

Three Billy Goats Gruff

Rumpelstiltskin

Jack and the Beanstalk

Puss in Boots

BALL GAMES

What is your favorite ball game to play?
What is your favorite ball game to watch?
Which game would you like to learn to play?
Which game have you never played?

soccer

baseball

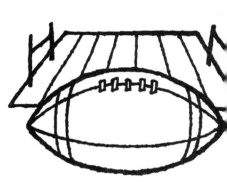

football

basketball

volleyball

dodgeball

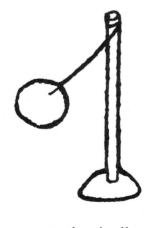

tetherball

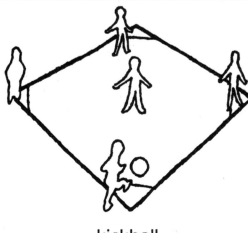

kickball

Ping Pong

ACTIVITIES

What is your favorite summer activity?
What is your favorite winter activity?
What do you like to do with your family? with friends?
Which activity have you never tried?

ice skating

sledding

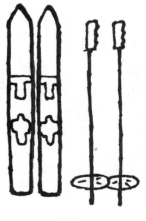

skiing

picnicking

reading

building snowmen

playground

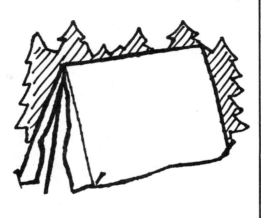

camping

swimming

WEATHER

What is the weather today?
Is today hot, cold, or mild?
What weather will we have most this month?

sunny

cloudy

rainy

snowy

foggy

windy

cold

hot

mild

WEATHER • CLOUDS • SEASONS

Is today a lion or a lamb day? (for a March graph)

Which kind of cloud is in the sky today?

What season is this month in?

Which season do you like best?

lion day

lamb day

cirrus

stratus

nimbus

cumulus

spring

summer

fall

SEASONS • MAGNETS • BUOYANCY • PROBABILITY

Will this object sink or float?
When you toss the coin, does it land heads or tails?
Does the magnet attract this object or not?
Is this animal a plant-eater or a meat-eater?

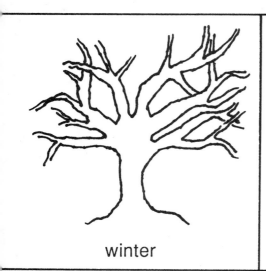

winter

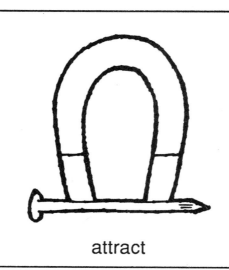

attract

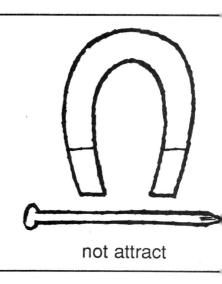

not attract

sink

float

heads

tails

meat-eater

plant-eater

PREHISTORIC LIFE • NATURAL HISTORY

What is your favorite prehistoric animal?
To what group does this animal belong?
Which group of animals makes the best pets?
From which animal groups do we get our food?

apatosaurus

icthyosaurus

triceratops

stegosaurus

pterodactyl

tyrannosaurus

mammals

amphibians

reptiles

NATURAL HISTORY

How many different animals can you think of from this group?
From which group are most of the animals in our classroom/school?
Which group has your favorite kinds of animals?
Which groups live mostly in water? on land?

birds

fish

insects

arachnids

crustaceans

warm-blooded

cold-blooded

vertebrates

invertebrates

LEAVES • SHAPES

Let's sort these leaves by shape.

Which leaf shape is most common?

Which shape has the most colorful leaves?

Let's sort these objects by shape.

What shape of cracker do you like best?

 smooth	 lobed	 pointed
 serrated	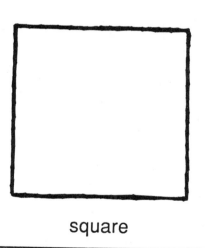 square	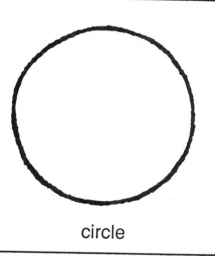 circle
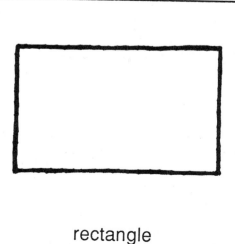 triangle	rectangle	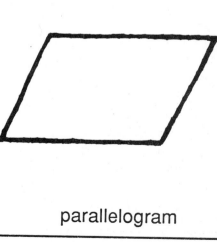 parallelogram

SHAPES • BUTTONS

Let's sort these shapes by numbers of sides.
Which shapes did you use in your design?
What shapes are most common in the classroom? on the
   playground?
Let's sort the buttons by number of holes.

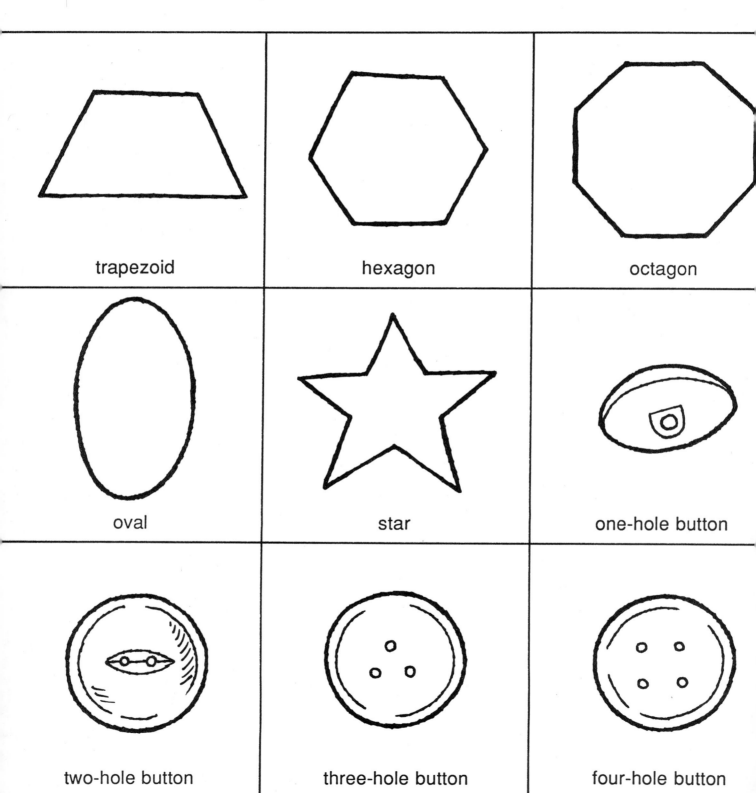

trapezoid

hexagon

octagon

oval

star

one-hole button

two-hole button

three-hole button

four-hole button

Index